FAMILY AT WORK

Building Strong Relationships at Home

James R. Kok

CRC Publications
Grand Rapids, Michigan

The discussion suggestions that accompany each chapter were prepared by Beverely Y. Muffin, Director of Language Communications for Evangelism at the Crystal Cathedral in Garden Grove, California.

Library of Congress Cataloging-in-Publication Data
Kok, James R., 1935-
    Family at work: building strong relationships at home /
James R. Kok.
        p.   cm.
    ISBN 1-56212-398-X
    1. Family—Religious aspects—Christianity. 2. Parenting—
Religious aspects—Christianity. 3. Marriage—Religious aspects—
Christianity. 4. Family—United States—Religious life.
I. Title.
BV4526.2.K65   1999
248.4—dc21   99-21262
                                                 CIP

0 9 8 7 6 5 4 3 2 1

CONTENTS

PREFACE

Courage, or something like it, is needed to write about the family. I feel about as confident setting out thoughts in this arena as I would writing about golf. Only a consistent professional ought to do that, and I feel high excellence in neither golf nor shaping families. But I work at both.

These chapters are more like sharing the "aha's" of many years of trying to get it right. Usually, but not always, an "aha" occurs when we hit a pothole on the highway of daily travel. Those unwelcome jolts have a way of getting our attention and ushering in a fresh way of seeing things. I pass along some of my discoveries in the hope that some readers will glean good insights from them before a pothole jostles them into learning readiness.

Raising a child takes a lot of thought. No longer can this most vital of all endeavors be accomplished well just by doing what comes naturally. Trusting the village to raise the child is risky as society plunges headlong into runaway secularism and materialism. The values of even close friends often veer in directions we may view as shallow or careless.

Today's parents need concerted personal energy to monitor use of the television and personal computer. Careful decision-making must control dressing the children in a way that props up their self-esteem without buying into the market and peer pressures wholesale. Canny planning must direct food preparation and consumption now that we know so much more about nutritional benefits. Even waste disposal and conservation of resources call for thoughtfulness. Spiritual nurturing, the most important component of all, demands time and strength every day. Many more areas could be added to this list of critical concerns that do not happen automatically in raising a child.

As a result, conscientious parents can no longer do justice to hand-fuls of children. Only a uniquely gifted few can nurture the large families of yesteryear the way they should be nurtured today. Why the change? Our culture offers so many considerations and opportu-nities to each individual child that parents need to spend far more time managing the lives of their offspring than they did in past decades. Also, today's parents want to have close personal relation-ships with their children. This is a newer value—highly appropriate, greatly rewarding, but somewhat puzzling to former generations more bent on being fruitful and multiplying than on enjoying their offspring as friends.

Large or small, families need help. This book is offered in the spirit of enabling this precious process a little bit. As an adoring grandfather, I now see more clearly how busy we were just taking care of the logistics of getting four children the essentials as we saw them. I wish now I had read more, reflected more, taken more time, stood back and pondered more about what those little kids needed.

The biggest gift we give to our children is character. Character includes the integrity and the capacity to set boundaries. It includes a depth dimension that shines with generosity and gratitude. Above all, character exhibits itself in living beyond the pleasure principal. It shows itself in building, working, creating, and caring, generated by strong confidence that God cares, needs, and appreciates lives dedicated to making the world a better place. If anything in these chapters facilitates that kind of living in even one person, the investment put into these pages is worthwhile.

—James R. Kok

1

LOVE OF FAMILY SHOWS LOVE OF GOD

Spiritual health has more to do with taking care of key relationships than with devotional practices. Vital faith builds bridges and connects people.

Joy Belc is troubled. She is a devout Christian who married her athletic high school sweetheart. In their courtship years they were active together in young adult programs at the church in which they both grew up. Their wedding was a lovely, traditional Protestant ceremony, and Joy anticipated living happily ever after.

Shortly after they settled into their new home, an unexpected change took place. Mike announced on a Friday evening that he was going to the desert on Saturday with some guys. They owned all-terrain vehicles and had invited him to spend the weekend with them challenging the hills and arroyos of the wilderness. Joy was welcome to come along too, since the other wives were going.

As the months passed, more and more weekends were devoted to desert, mountain, or beach outings. Joy loved these outings but was increasingly uneasy that they were missing church so much. She raised the issue with Mike, but he breezed over it.

A low level of dissonance began to grow in Joy. Something was wrong. She knew it was the erosion of her values, the lost routine of church attendance and the spiritual refocusing it provided. So she resolved to drop out of the weekend adventures, even though Mike refused. She was convinced that God wanted her in church.

Mike and Joy's separate tracks deepened. She began to nag. He responded with anger, claiming she was deserting him. Joy visited a therapist.

Counsel encouraged Joy's resolve to work out a compromise. So Joy launched a tremendously determined confrontation. When the tears dried and tempers cooled, she and Mike had agreed on a fifty-fifty proposition. Half of the weekends would be outings and half would be spent at home and church.

What broke Joy's determined stand was the fresh insight that working to ensure that her marriage stayed strong and satisfying was a primary Christian duty. If Mike wouldn't move, she would have to compromise.

Not all of us would feel comfortable with Joy and Mike's week-on, week-off lifestyle. Some would not accept less than 100 percent

Lord's Day observance. But in a world in which most Christians rarely or never go to church, 50 percent is a lot.

This young woman's struggle and trade-off illustrate a reality that traditional Christians need to think about—the reality that marriage is not secondary to the usual top-drawer spiritual activities such as Bible study, prayer, tithing, volunteer service, or church attendance. Activities that weaken or threaten a marriage, while ostensibly serving the Lord, need to be reconsidered. All play or all worship are equally dangerous if a marriage is at stake.

On several occasions I have met with troubled spouses of seminary students. Usually their problem boiled down to being left alone, evening after evening, as their husbands or wives studied theology—first at the library and then deep into the night at home.

When asked why they didn't protest, each would point out that they couldn't do that because their husbands/wives were busy doing "God's work."

Because I was a pastor myself, it was easy to deliver a convincing sermon to them about marriage as one of God's highest priorities. I strongly urged the neglected spouses to act as radically as necessary to alter this misguided behavior of their young husbands or wives.

It is not uncommon to see another version of the seminarian scenario in which one spouse wades deeper and deeper into prayer groups and Bible study. For some these activities become an addiction—everything else seems unimportant. As a result, an unbridgeable chasm opens between husband and wife, parent and child. I am sure the Lord cringes when time and adoration are abstractly focused on him while marriage and family are nearly ignored. A life of piety must strengthen, not weaken, marriage and other important relationships.

Marriage is the foundation of our society. It must not be taken for granted. People who put maximum energy into their employment err if they only give leftovers at home. Creative men and women who star in the marketplace must generate equal inventiveness with home and family. Christians who hold the Lord above all others demonstrate it by proper family life, not by Bible study.

Without Christ at the center of one's life, self-serving is understandable, and a lackadaisical approach to marriage isn't so surprising. But Christians are told that neglecting one's spouse (and children) is akin to neglecting the Lord himself. Those who are busy in church work and activities commonly regarded as serving the Lord have another guess coming if they justify marital or familial negligence in the process (see Song of Solomon 1:6, "They made me keeper of the vineyards; but my own vineyard I have not kept!").

If we want to do what is right, we will strive for a well-balanced mix of church activities and ardent devotion to building and maintaining marriage and family. That's what Christian wedding vows commit us to, pure and simple. And because marriage is God's idea, keeping those vows will be abundantly rewarding and personally satisfying.

SCRIPTURE REFLECTIONS

TITUS 2:3-4

> *. . . teach what is good, so that they may encourage the young women to love their husbands, to love their children. . . .*

1. How can young women show their love for their husbands in difficult situations?

2. What are some pre-difficulty love foundations that should be in place in a marriage?

TITUS 2:6-7

> *Likewise, urge the younger men to be self-controlled. Show yourselves in all respects a model of good works. . . .*

1. How do young husbands fall into inconsiderate ways?

2. How do you learn to "give" in difficult situations without feeling resentful?

TITUS 3:8

The saying is sure.

I desire that you insist on these things, so that those who have come to believe in God may be careful to devote themselves to good works; these things are excellent and profitable to everyone.

1. What are some "good works" wives should perform?

2. What are some "good works" husbands should perform?

PERSONAL REFLECTIONS

1. Rate yourself on the following on a scale of 1-5 (1=completely agree, 5=completely disagree):

It is easy for me to give in to my spouse. ___

My parents' marriage was a good example for me. ___

I dislike being told what to do. ___

I only think ideas are good if they're mine. ___

I am quick to say "I'm sorry" and mean it. ___

I am always taking a stand for what I think is right. ___

I'm pleasant, even if I'm not having my way. ___

I just can't be pleasant and give in to my partner. ___

I feel wronged if my partner demands to do things his/her way. ___

I want my partner to be with me at all times. ___

I cannot live with fifty-fifty arrangements. ___

2. What are some good compromises

- when one party wants to do one thing, and the other party another?

- when one party goes to church on Sunday and the other party does not want to go to church?

- when interests are extremely different?

3. If you are married

- plan an outing to please the husband.

  What _____

  Where _____

  When _____

  Results _____

- plan an outing to please the wife.

  What _____

  Where _____

  When _____

  Results _____

If you are not married

- plan an outing to please another person.

  What _____

  Where _____

  When _____

  Results _____

2

MARRIAGE, AFTER THE ROCKETS HAVE DROPPED AWAY

yths and mirages of marriage do a lot to sow discontent among determined partners. Reality, sensible expectations, and reasonable goals and objectives pave the way for stable, secure commitments that last.

Someone jostled me recently, asking why I seldom write about marriage. The question made me wonder too.

My facetious-sounding answer declared the truth: "Because I haven't figured it out yet." Nevertheless, effectively prodded, I will share some of my observations from personal experience after thirty years of marriage.

1. Marriage Takes Hard Work.

When a man and a woman join together in marriage, a unique arrangement commences. On the one hand, a strong physical and psychological attraction pulls them irresistibly toward each other. On the other hand, these two experience life in almost opposite ways: men and women think, talk, solve problems, and relate to others differently. Developing a satisfying, mutual relationship between such unique puzzle parts is a lifelong challenge. But when a husband and wife finally synchronize their systems, something wonderful happens.

2. Feelings Change.

Passion lifts marriage off the ground. Physical and emotional excitement about each other works like powerful rockets boosting a capsule into space. Once orbit is achieved, the power packs of desire and attraction drop away. Then the daunting work of building a secure home and healthy family begins. Little rockets still ignite to keep the ship on course, but the big ones are gone forever. After the launch, marriage depends on promises kept. The solid satisfactions unique to a permanent, secure, and reliable connection to another, through the ups and downs of life's flight, add needed glue. The original excitement must settle into stable, ordinary, homemaking love.

3. Conflict Inevitably Arises.

"Accept me as I am," pleads each partner in marriage. But the long process whereby two become one demands a lot of rubbing of rough edge against rough edge. The oneness spoken of in the wedding ceremony is largely in the mind of God at that point. Time, conflict, problem-solving, working, praying, and playing together gradually accomplish the grooving that melds man and woman into a unified whole. The special rewards marriage holds are available in a unique way to those who spend decades rubbing and bumping each other until the rough spots are smooth and the fit is sweet.

Occasionally couples claim to have a conflict-free union. Either these are extremely rare combinations of compatibility or one of the two is perpetually giving in. A shriveled partner who goes along with everything is not the helper God calls him or her to be. When one constantly concedes to the other, mutual growth stops and a relationship of imbalance sets in. Calm may reign in that household, but it comes at the expense of true unity, godly equality, and intentional mutuality. These valued conditions require controlled conflict, enlightened negotiating, and careful compromise.

4. Rituals and Routines Help.
Feelings are unpredictable and unreliable deliverers of intimacy. My wife, Linda, and I habitually kiss goodbye as she leaves for her teaching work each morning and I head for my office. The routine includes her standing on the six-inch step up out of our kitchen to equalize our height a little. We do this whether we feel like it or not. The sacramental nature of the daily connection works its blessing on both of us. Good stuff flows even when our minds stick on the tasks of the day instead of personal affection.

We also touch or hold hands ritually for times of prayer—in church and at other occasions, including mealtime devotions. Habit and commitment keep this going. Feelings change too much.

Physical and sexual intimacy so blesses life together that leaving it up to feelings is too chancy. Routines and regular times agreed upon and calendared guarantee the steady benefits of closeness and caring.

5. Time Together Brings Benefits.
Linda and I begin each day with an hour of *L.A. Times* and KUSC radio; formal breakfast times have been scrapped since the children departed. Then we go our separate working ways. We try to come together for a forty-five minute walk along the San Gabriel River each day before dark.

These two hours seal the companionship and unity of our lives, providing pleasant catching up and debriefing opportunities for our separate daily pressures and joys. The other twenty-two hours may hold large or small chunks of togetherness, but often they do not. Keeping the two special times holy yields a unique bonding benefit we both cherish.

6. Love Without God Wears Thin.

Life is tough. Satisfactions and joys abound, but loss, failure, pressures, responsibilities, and uncontrollable situations trickle relentlessly into every family. Conscientiously connecting to the Source of all love and goodness helps keep relationships from foundering on the shoals of hard times.

To keep that connection strong, a Christ-centered environment is important, a place where people talk about vital relational ideas such as resurrection, forgiveness, faithfulness, compassion, justice, fairness, patience, hospitality, encouragement, and long-suffering. Church attendance, small groups, and friendships with those sharing these values nourish struggling souls and challenge languishing marriages toward creative solutions. In the Christian community, a Holy Spirit generates and fuels vital therapeutic energy transmitted in part by loving human contact. The spread of this healing electricity into our marriages spot-welds a lot of stress fractures.

The weekly hours of refueling and refocusing together on Sunday may be the strongest marital fastener of our time. We neglect them at our peril and participate to our bountiful benefit.

SCRIPTURE REFLECTIONS

SONG OF SOLOMON 2:10-13

My beloved speaks and says to me:

"Arise, my love, my fair one,
*   and come away;*
for now the winter is past,
*   the rain is over and gone.*
The flowers appear on the earth;
*   the time of singing has come,*
and the voice of the turtledove
*   is heard in our land.*
The fig tree puts forth its figs,
*   and the vines are in blossom;*
*   they give forth fragrance.*
Arise, my love, my fair one,
*   and come away!"*

1. **What are some of the circumstances of life that cause us to forget to "come away" and set time apart for our marriages?**

2. **How can we keep our priorities in place and make time for marriage enrichment?**

PROVERBS 5:18

Let your fountain be blessed,
and rejoice in the wife of your youth. . . .

1. What are the blessings of marriage?

2. How do they outweigh the problems of marriage?

3. List at least ten good qualities of your marriage, or someone's you admire:

_____   _____

_____   _____

_____   _____

_____   _____

_____   _____

4. How are these qualities attained?

PERSONAL REFLECTIONS

In the following questions, use your own experience with marriage. (If you're not married, use examples of marriages you've observed.)

1. What are some areas of "hard work" common to most marriages?

2. List some good results of "hard work" in marriage.

3. List several mature "feelings" that come as a couple works at marriage. What are some good "changes" that result from working at marriage?

4. Why is "Accept me as I am" such a difficult accomplishment?

5. Think of three innovative rituals that can bring a couple closer together:

_____

_____

_____

6. What are you looking for in companionship?

   How are you finding it?

7. How is a marriage helped by "Christian community"?

8. What part do valuable friends play in helping to keep a marriage strong?

9. Suggest some good ideas for "refueling" a marriage.

3

WHO CAN CLEAN A DIRTY SINK?

Almost everybody resists change. But just the fact that change upsets us and evokes unsettled feelings does not mean the new way is wrong. Growth requires giving up old ways and entering a period of discomfort before improvement emerges.

The Spirit of God never stops leading us onward and upward. New plateaus serve as launching places for further advances. Trust in God's faithfulness encourages us to venture into life's exciting uncharted territories.

I will never forget the moment a new microchip clicked into place in my brain. I had entered our tiny green bathroom, but my hands cringed at the dirtiness of the wash basin where forty filthy little fingers had made their offerings. As I exited, a flash of fresh insight electrified my system: *"I can clean that sink!"* Modern young couples may gasp with disbelief that anyone would require a special revelation for something so obvious.

Other role-modifying experiences had already challenged me: "Change the baby's diaper" and "It's your turn to get up with the baby." But those came from my wife and always felt like temporary assistance with hard tasks that really belonged to her.

My conversion in the green room snapped something. A wall crumbled that day. Dirty sinks were suddenly *our* project whereas before they had been Linda's alone. Of course, I was not totally remodeled on the spot. My mind changed. But behavior waddles reluctantly along, trying to catch up with the brain.

Although young Christians marrying in the '80s and '90s have embraced marital mutuality, some traditional division of labor endures in their homes too: he changes the car's oil, she handles the wash. But more and more young people tackle tasks together rather than falling back on old patterns of "woman's work" or "man's work."

Not long ago I enjoyed sleeping overnight in the home of our son and his wife. As I dressed for my speaking engagement, I found my shirt badly crunched from eight hours in a garment bag. Instinctively I said to daughter-in-law Carol, "Would you mind pressing my shirt a little? It's awfully wrinkled." Before she could answer, my son said, "Here, I'll do it, Dad." I gulped with enlightened chagrin. (The next step forward calls for me to iron it myself.)

The generation gap deepened that day. He irons all his own shirts, I learned, as she pursues her education and works as a field geologist. I contemplated whether or not to bring this story home to my hard-working schoolteacher wife. We follow rather traditional patterns when it comes to the ironing board.

My meager progress toward mutuality embarrasses me. I now grocery shop and prepare a major meal or two each week, but old habits prevail. Nevertheless I strongly believe in, and teach, division of labor along the lines of skill, interest, and availability—not tradition—to young folks contemplating matrimony. This, I am convinced, is God's script for modern Christians.

Christian marriage prospers when husband and wife love the other as themselves—when they look for opportunities to encourage growth and development in each other. One is not to shrink while his or her partner expands. Each seeks the delicate balance of giving and receiving, serving and being served, as both find ways to use their talents and carry their share of the load.

In marriages of mutuality, household tasks are, when physically possible, shared. In my marriage some of this mutuality has evolved, even though it's contrary to the roles we saw modeled in the homes in which we grew up. For example, for most of our thirty years, Linda, a more careful and thrifty person than I, has balanced our checkbook. Giving up the macho power of managing our money threatened me at first. But soon good sense prevailed. My masculinity fragmented temporarily, but our financial affairs firmed up. Now we're both happy.

In ages past, each day served up ample satisfying work for husband and wife. He worked the farm or the factory. She easily filled the daylight hours with shopping, cleaning, cooking, and childcare. Both owned clearly defined roles. Education and the simplification of home chores eventually modified that neat arrangement. Many young women crave broader intellectual challenges and the opportunities to earn and handle marketplace challenges. Young men increasingly covet the personal satisfactions of childcare and culinary craftsmanship. Happily, more now plot and plan for their roles to be interchangeable.

Although some of today's Christian youth maintain remnants of traditional headship patterns, many young Christian couples today put little stress on head-of-the-house issues. They prefer instead, and practice well, shared headship. Each, in his or her own way, endeavors to be a helper, nurturer, advocate, mediator, colleague, and facilitator. One looks out for the good of the other. Instead of waxing nostalgic for the good old days of strong family values, we might better take inventory of what is really going on. A majority of contemporary Christian homes are vibrant centers of teamwork modeling superior moral health and value-laden vitality. Many surpass in excellence the families from which they have sprung. Some of us can take lessons from our children while congratulating ourselves that they operate so smartly.

SCRIPTURE REFLECTIONS

JOHN 13:3-5

Jesus, knowing that the Father had given all things into his hands, and that he had come from God and was going to God, got up from the table, took off his outer robe, and tied a towel around himself. Then he poured water into a basin and began to wash the disciples' feet and to wipe them with the towel that was tied around him.

1. List some characteristics of a servant-leader (include several you see in Jesus).

2. List some servant-leader characteristics of the following:

Men

Women

Husbands

Wives

Christians

PERSONAL REFLECTIONS

1. Be honest about your preconceived ideas.

Women should do:

Men should do:

_____   _____

_____   _____

_____   _____

_____   _____

_____   _____

2. How do some of your ideas need "role-modifying"?

3. How can we encourage growth and development in our spouse?

4. List some of the qualities of a person you know and admire.

Woman Servant-Leader   Man Servant-Leader

_____   _____

_____   _____

_____   _____

_____   _____

_____   _____

5. What are your best servant-leader qualities?

4

DEATH MUST NOT WIN

"*Pick yourself up.*
Dust yourself off.
Start all over again."

(Popular song—Christian mandate)

S pencer and Molly Gardener cruised to a happy start in their married life. Both held satisfying jobs, experienced good health, and embraced strong values supported by their faith. After five years in the marketplace, they agreed to start a family. True to form for them, babies came easily and healthfully. Soon there were three.

When Spencer and Molly had been married fourteen busy but happy years, their children were ages nine, seven, and three. Then the incredible swept in. Within twenty-four months tragic accidents took the lives of the oldest and youngest.

No heartbreak equals the death of one's child. Two defies all comprehension. Only God can fathom and feel the depth of grief in Spencer and Molly. They went on, but never came close to getting on with life in a moderately happy way.

When the surviving child, Anne, reached mature adulthood, she reflected on life in the Gardener household after the deaths of her siblings. Following the tragedies, she said, joy never returned. Anne stayed at home until age twenty without ever again seeing zest, excitement, or vitality in her parents' lives. Her own ongoing life provided little solace to them. Her many accomplishments brought minimal comfort.

Death had taken two children—*and their parents*. Only Anne survived. Death had won.

Death wins whenever small or large catastrophes, small or large failures, disappointments, and setbacks make a lasting negative impact on anyone's life. Grief, sorrow, and heartache are normal, even necessary. Every loss is a death. Every loss takes a toll. Nevertheless, Christian living insists on resurrection. Death must not have the last word.

Death comes in many forms: the disappointments of rejection in career aspirations, the handicaps of one's child or self, the failure of faith in a loved one, hopes for marriage dashed, business setbacks, being left out of something desired, making a serious mistake—the list stretches endlessly beyond these few examples. All are death-like experiences.

It is irritating and worrisome to those who have experienced "death" for disappointments and losses to be glossed over too lightly, as if they are "nothing at all." But it is sad beyond words when deaths—small or big—permanently dispirit, indelibly sour, irreversibly embitter. Never making a comeback is contrary to Christ's resurrection spirit. Death stands triumphant when the body remains in the tomb.

Arnold and Mary live with an ongoing agony. A beloved and talented child now resides in the foggy, confused, fantasy world of psychosis. Her presence in the home makes the tragedy a daily reality they cannot ignore even for a day or two.

Some long nights both Arnold and Mary lie awake wondering, wishing, and weeping. And they will never stop praying that an exit door will open, allowing their daughter to leave her unreal world and return to normalcy. But Arnold and Mary are alive and well anyway. They enjoy life. They work. They play. Their friends and faith are meaningful and fulfilling. The death of their daughter's health and future is a living fatality, but it has not won. The mental illness, though agonizingly sad, has not drained away their zest and joy.

People give up over far less:

- Hal Swenson wanted to be a journalist, but after failing to gain admission to the top school in the country, he took a night job in a twenty-four-hour gas station. He's still there, a grim character, twenty years later.

- Margaret Tracy's life ended when her beauty shop, uninsured, burned. Twelve years later she talks of little else, works part-time for a former competitor, blames others, complains bitterly.

- Bert was swindled heartlessly by his partner. At age forty-five he found himself empty-handed, all his possessions and savings claimed by creditors. His spirit went too. Today, eight years later, no evidence of recovery or a comeback is in sight. Ailments keep multiplying—a consequence, one conjectures, of his broken heart.

Stories like these are not as well-known as are their opposites. They never make *Guideposts* and *Possibilities,* for obvious reasons. Dramatic reversals of misfortune get published. They inspire and ignite our own depleted energies, helping the flattened to rise again. Too common are the times where one death leads to another, when roadblocks become dead ends instead of detours to another way. Too often a rejection marks the occasion for suicide of the spirit or cancer of the soul.

Resurrections must keep happening! Rebirths signify the spirit of Christianity. Barrenness turned to life is a constant theme in Scripture. Vitality is a precious gift not to be wasted or given up. The spirit of Christ overcomes death, rises again, defeats the Enemy. The Enemy wants us to believe there is no future. The Enemy uses small deaths and major tragedies to whisper to us that we live in a hope-less world. "Curse God and die," suggests the Tempter when dreams lie shattered.

But the Christian outlook always strives to be hopeful. Even when temporarily depressed by whatever dismaying circumstance comes our way, we need to see hope waiting in the wings. Easter is always just down the way a little. Death must not win!

The spirit of hope sings its lovely song in these words of St. Paul:

> We are afflicted in every way, but not crushed; perplexed, but not driven to despair; persecuted, but not forsaken; struck down, but not destroyed (2 Cor. 4:8-9).

Displaying this outlook to our children is crucial Christian living. Children usually exude a natural God-given resilience. They bounce back quickly from adversity. But living with dispirited adults, deplet-ed of hope, will gradually inject children and teens with soul-sickening despair.

The caring friends of those struck down must refuse to let them sink down to die. Battered souls must be supported, encouraged, and resuscitated by persistent and prolonged deliverers of spiritual first aid. Though struck down, they must not be destroyed.

Christians are witnesses to and carriers of resurrection hope. Life can begin again. Starting over is possible. After mourning, joy can dawn afresh. But Christians also know that there is no resurrection without death, no real hope without first hopelessness, no true happiness unless sorrow is also known. Superficial joy won't do. Joy that glosses over heartaches is hollow. Jesus' own joy included, as an essential ingredient, a trip to hell and back. Only those struck down are equipped to be witnesses to resurrection. Only those who have been hard-pressed on every side have the credibility to speak of life after death.

The resurrection of Jesus is testimony to the presence of the living God in this world, overshadowing the power of darkness. Ever-present, the same revitalizing Spirit that raised Jesus from the dead refreshes and renews his people, gets them going again.

SCRIPTURE REFLECTIONS

2 CORINTHIANS 4:8-9

We are afflicted in every way, but not crushed; perplexed, but not driven to despair; persecuted, but not forsaken; struck down, but not destroyed.

Restate this Scripture in your own words, as it applies to you.

2 CORINTHIANS 4:16

So we do not lose heart.

List some things you do or think to keep you from despair in life's circumstances.

2 CORINTHIANS 4:18

. . . because we look not at what can be seen but at what cannot be seen; for what can be seen is temporary, but what cannot be seen is eternal.

What are several of your eternal values?

ISAIAH 12:2-3

Surely God is my salvation;
I will trust, and will not be afraid,
for the LORD GOD is my strength and my might;
he has become my salvation.
With joy you will draw water from the wells of salvation.

1. **Why is it sometimes so difficult to trust the Lord and not be afraid?**

2. **How do we draw water from the "wells of salvation"?**

PERSONAL REFLECTIONS

1. Describe one of your "death-like" experiences.

2. How did Christ's resurrection spirit affect that experience?

   How long did it take; what was the process?

3. Is there a situation in which you need the resurrection spirit today?

   What is needed for you to experience that spirit?

4. If you were dealing with a person needing an experience of resurrection

   What would you say to them?

   What advice might you give them?

   What Scripture might you offer them?

   How would you pray for them?

5

INVOLVED DADS PRODUCE BETTER KIDS

A man's diligence in actively nurturing his children outweighs all else in importance. The responsible man sets nearly all else slightly below this priority.

Children need mothering *and* fathering to grow up well. Traditionally, mothering supplies warmth, nurturing, and unconditional acceptance. Mothering embraces, comforts, and reassures—no matter what. Mothering is there, freely given, available in times of failure and delinquency as well as in times of success and compliance. To be mothered is to be listened to, touched, held, and wept with.

Fathering traditionally acts more conditionally. Fathering pushes toward excelling. Fathering demands performance, measuring up. Fathering expects the job to be done before praise is given. Fathering encourages going a little farther, working hard, taking risks, acting bravely, living with excitement. To be fathered is to have a model of physical strength, firmness, consistency, law and order.

In the intact home in which both husband and wife are present, they usually, together, provide all the necessary qualities of mothering and fathering. Significant fathering qualities may be present in the woman. Some of the mothering attributes may be more developed in the man. In unison, the needed balance emerges—conditional acceptance and unconditional love, softness and toughness, emotion and reason, vulnerability and invulnerability. For the most part, women and men complement each other along the lines traditionally seen as male and female. He brings what she lacks. She makes up for his deficiencies.

The importance of the traditional father's contribution to the well-being of his children has long been severely undervalued. Mother's presence and care have appropriately been given sky-high ratings, but Father's role in the everyday lives of his children has nearly been regarded as superfluous. He serves as the breadwinner while Mother raises the children. The strong arm of discipline may come from Dad, but this role has been routinely discounted as merely a needed control factor that prevents chaos and preserves order. The truth is that children grow up best when Father is present, available, responsive, and exhibiting qualities that are often present in men and complementary to women—qualities like playfulness, physical robustness, power, adventurousness, courage, discipline.

The Christian community, deeply invested in its children, must be terribly concerned for the fatherless (and motherless). Support for single parents—those who must blaze the difficult path of being both mother and father to their offspring—is crucial. Being all that a dad and mom should be dearly challenges the most gifted individual. Compassion, understanding, prayers, and encouragement must flow for all who bear this responsibility alone. Finding creative ways of making up for some of the gaps in the one-parent family is a reasonable and necessary obligation for friends, relatives, and the church.

Our Lord and Creator is the complete parent. All the attributes we see as belonging to a father are present in God. Everything we value in a mother is clearly there too. On the one hand there is law: "Measure up or else!" On the other hand, "I'll love you even when you fail." "Thou shalt not!" and "Come unto me you who are weary and heavily burdened" coexist. There is dispassionate expectation along with unfathomable compassion: "Be perfect!" but "Though your sins be as scarlet, they shall be as white as snow."

The vital balance—fathering and mothering, power and presence, toughness and tenderness—exists in our loving God.

Whatever else those blessed with children are called to do in this world, nothing equals the vocation of being a parent. If we are totally successful in the business world, in a profession, or as a keeper of a clean house, but miss the mark with our children, what good is all the other? If we are mediocre or even below average in our employment but bring up just one well-adjusted, world-enhancing, God-pleasing child, we are fantastically successful.

If you are a father, wake up afresh to the importance of your child-rearing mission. Examine your lifestyle, habits, and patterns, and make the changes needed to bring yourself more intimately into the hands-on parenting picture. Unless there are reciprocal agreements, there is no place for the traditional night out with the boys. Long prime-time golf outings and hunting expeditions should be restructured or postponed until the children can participate. Enjoying "couch potato" passivity while Mother reads to the children and prepares them for bed should be an obsolete luxury, gone forever.

Jesus had strong warnings about causing a little one to stumble. Today's research is pointing increasingly to the role of fathers in molding and modeling for children. Faltering youth relate closely to failing fathers. Healthy, wholesome young people usually have actively involved dads. Law-keeping children reflect the presence of a father in the home, leading and influencing.

The Christian community gets higher-than-average grades in family life values and performance. But there is ample room for fathers' improvement. The rewards are well worth the effort.

SCRIPTURE REFLECTIONS

MATTHEW 19:14

But Jesus said, "Let the little children come to me, and do not stop them; for it is to such as these that the kingdom of heaven belongs."

1. In what ways do we sometimes severely undervalue children?

2. How would you see children according to the values of Jesus?

GENESIS 27:26-27

Then his father Isaac said to him, "Come near and kiss me, my son." So he came near and kissed him; and he smelled the smell of his garments, and blessed him, and said:

"Ah, the smell of my son
is like the smell of a field that the LORD has blessed."

1. Often, fathers avoid tender emotions with their children. Why?

2. How can fathers show tenderness to their children?

2 TIMOTHY 1:5

I am reminded of your sincere faith, a faith that lived first in your grandmother Lois and your mother Eunice and now, I am sure, lives in you.

How can extended families and significant others help one parent or both parents in the parenting of children?

PERSONAL REFLECTIONS

1. **Review the importance of some "historically"
   appropriate father/mother roles on a scale of 1-5
   (1=least valuable, 5=most valuable):**

   Fathers do yard work and carry out the trash. ____

   Mothers do dishes. ____

   Fathers tend to family autos. ____

   Mothers tend to the sick and change diapers. ____

   Fathers lead family devotions. ____

   Mothers hear bedtime prayers. ____

   Fathers supervise family sports. ____

   Mothers clean house. ____

   Fathers attend to family trusts, wills, stocks. ____

   Mothers pay the bills. ____

2. **Can you suggest several better "together" ways of doing
   things?**

3. **How can men and women complement each other?**

4. What are some ways in which the church family can help in single parenting?

5. What are some ways the church family can help in general parenting?

6. If you are a parent, what are some of your best parenting values? If you are not a parent, what parenting values do you admire?

6

TRUST IS CAUGHT MORE THAN TAUGHT

"*Do your best and let God do the rest.*"

Rose Benedict impatiently scolded her two-and-a-half-year-old daughter: "You have to fold your hands and close your eyes to pray to God before you eat, Lisa. If you don't, God won't be happy with you." Then Rose softly but sternly slapped Lisa's errant fingers.

The God of Scripture promises to be a loving and faithful presence in our children's lives and ours, but sometimes, like Rose, we lose confidence and act as though we have to force our children into an appropriate response. We forget that few things in life go well when forced—spiritual growth least of all.

Accepting God's promises implies living in a way that reflects this trust to our children. Modeling trust eliminates the necessity to nag, prod, coerce, and scare children into a posture of faith. Modeling goes slower but works better.

Training Lisa to close her eyes and fold her hands for prayer makes sense. But Rose seems so anxious, urgent, and panicky about her discipline. She communicates fear of God and the idea that God is mostly legalistic and punitive. And she acts as if she alone is entrusted with the awesome responsibility of making her little girl into a Christian.

That's not how it should be in homes where parents have received the promises of God. Lisa is a child of the promise. God has given his word to take care of her. Rose does not need to slap and chide her daughter into a life of gratitude. Lisa will learn thankfulness from her parents' grateful living.

Some of us live as if we—by our own hard work, cleverness, and skill—have to make life come out right. Often we do pretty well, accumulating achievements, earnings, security, and possessions. Our successes, however, feed an illusion that we can control life. And so we approach our children in the same "do-it-yourself" frame of mind. We begin to act as if it's up to us to make them into Christians by the direct approach, like Rose's patty slapping.

This attitude travels from generation to generation. Rose Benedict, for example, had herself been coerced and threatened into a Christian lifestyle by parents who had accomplished much by their hard work and determination. Rose emerged as one of their successful productions. Now she is determinedly hammering the next generation into shape.

Often, little of God's Spirit shines through in the lives of such driven people. They are Christians, but not saved from much. They are believers, but exhibit little faith. God promises, but they work it out themselves. They stomp on the promises instead of standing on them. In effect, they're saying, "It's okay, God. I'll manage for myself."

Such an attitude ignores God's promise to always be present to us and our children. Grateful fathers and mothers model for their children the spiritual security and settled peacefulness that this promise gives. Then our children will walk in God's ways without force or manipulation.

Trusting God loosens our grip and terminates the "white knuckle" approach to life that results from trying—with our own bare hands—to make our children turn out the way we want them to. There is a way of living and a way of raising our children that testifies to our reliance on God. This way, of course, includes discipline, training, high expectations, hard work, and all the other virtues we prize and need. But it also transmits a subtle yet solid confidence in God. This better way rests on God's promises and refuses to believe that it's up to us to pressure our children into the faith. "Let go and let God" says it well.

So Rose, relax! Lisa is in God's eternal embrace, and so are you. Rest in God's strong, caring hands. Release your frantic grip on the controls. God has control. And God has you. Encourage, inspire, enjoy Lisa. Train her, guide her, teach her. But most of all show her the way of resilient grace, cheerful freedom, and weatherproof hope that is yours as a child of promise.

What about the countless Christian parents who daily question both their own effectiveness and God's promises? Some mourn children who have radically departed from their early training.

Yes, God promises, but children do stray and go their own way. Disappointments, tragic human failures, and catastrophic personal loss litter our history. Temptation enters here. When we cannot figure it out, when it makes no sense, when there is no good in it, then we are tempted the most to retreat into hopelessness or into trying harder to fix things ourselves.

In such desperate times we must learn to trust God anyway. The empty-handedness of unexplainable losses and major failures can in fact get faith and trust on the right track better than smooth times and good fortune. Trust can reach new heights when, faced by blatant contradictions and mysterious perplexities, we still accept God's promise to be faithful.

Exceptions stick in our memories, teasing our confidence, but God is faithful. When Rose folds her own hands and serenely rests on God's promises, Lisa will fold in response. When Rose loosens her grip on Lisa and places her hands in God's, Lisa will come following after.

SCRIPTURE REFLECTIONS

1 JOHN 4:7-11

*Beloved, let us love one another, because love is from God;
everyone who loves is born of God and knows God. Whoever
does not love does not know God, for God is love. God's love was
revealed among us in this way: God sent his only Son into the
world so that we might live through him. In this is love, not that
we loved God but that he loved us and sent his Son to be the
atoning sacrifice for our sins. Beloved, since God loved us so
much, we also ought to love one another.*

EPHESIANS 2:8-9

*For by grace you have been saved through faith, and this is not
your own doing; it is the gift of God—not the result of works, so
that no one may boast.*

**1. Describe someone you know whose life speaks
   what he or she wants to teach. Give a few examples.**

2. How does his or her "modeling" affect you?

**3. Why do you think some people want to make
   Christianity so difficult? Describe some of the
   methods they use.**

PERSONAL REFLECTIONS

1. How can we be a part of spiritual growth in children?

2. Have you ever used "modeling" to influence others and help them grow? Describe what you did.

3. What makes us think we are the "creator" of children instead of God? How can we learn to rely more on God?

4. How can we be encouragers instead of discouragers? List two ways in which you will try to encourage someone in the next week.

5. List some of the promises of God in which we need to rest. (Consider 1 Peter 5:7, 2 Timothy 1:12, Matthew 19:14, Proverbs 22:6.)

7

WHAT MAKES YOU FEEL HAPPY?

Blessings and beauty abound. Why do we mostly notice the frustrations and irritations?

A group of people were asked to talk about what makes them feel angry. When they finished, they were asked to talk about what makes them feel happy. The first part flowed. The second stalled. Most found it much easier to specifically speak of that which frustrated, irritated, and exasperated:

- people who promise to call, but don't
- child abuse
- solitary drivers in the carpool lane
- smokers
- a car refusing to start
- nonstop talkers
- people who sell drugs

But trying to identify the sources and stimulants of positive feelings caused the group to falter and stammer. They could not rattle off lists neatly and exactly.

It made me think. Is happiness such a rarity that we can't pinpoint it easily? Are we really angry more than happy? The possibility depressed me. But as I continued to ponder the matter, I reached a pleasant conclusion. I realized that there are so many wonderful spirit-lifters, we glide right over them without paying appropriate attention. Anger marks interruptions and intrusions into our steady happiness stream. We notice the breakdowns and disruptions. Like an aluminum stepladder dropped in the middle of a flowing, crowded freeway, anger grabs all the attention. The rest of the rapid ride remains unremarkable.

One day last week our loaded, ready-to-brew coffeemaker failed to start automatically as programmed. Instead of awakening to the usual pleasant aroma and availability of fresh coffee, I glared at an empty pot. I was irritated. My daily gratification from the functioning pot had been stymied.

Happiness may not be the best word for simple joys like early-morning coffee. Maybe that term should be reserved for ultimate catechism concerns like "What is my only comfort in life and death?" Nevertheless I think there are showers of down-to-earth, everyday blessings that we may, loosely speaking, identify as bringing joy and happiness.

Kirk, whose spirit had been smothered by a deep depression, told how one day the depression mysteriously lifted, like a thick fog burned off by the sun. Everything became visible again. He noticed details like the veins on the leaves on the trees, the twittering of the sparrows, children playing, flowers, the blue sky. The expressions on people's faces gleamed exciting, beautiful, and full of vitality.

Thinking about what is palpably pleasurable can stimulate a heart-warming awakening to our surroundings. I share here my abridged list of everyday joy-generating, gratifying, pleasurable, happiness-producing sights, sounds, and events:

- my regular early-morning routine: reading and writing, looking out on our green and colorful backyard, drinking coffee accompanied, eventually, by my wife, who will share some of the newspaper highlights as we listen to public radio
- a twenty-foot row of gloriously multicolored impatiens bordering our patio
- the framed snapshots of our children and grandchildren on the bookcase
- a car that carries me reliably on the freeways
- a shuffle of octogenarians enjoying a potluck on our patio
- any action that preserves and cares for the environment
- a bunch of bikers—Asian, Anglo, and African American— passing on a nearby path
- people meeting loved ones at the airport with hugs, tears, smiles, and joy
- a freshly mowed lawn
- a teenage boy cuddling a cat
- sinking a difficult putt
- two people in a car, laughing
- two elderly women collecting aluminum cans in the park
- learning new, useable words like "oxymoron" and "segue"
- a telephone message thanking me for something I wrote
- rain

Definitely, the best things in life are free!

Acute shortages of oxygen, food, money, health, meaningful employment, friends, and shelter, of course, radically subdue one's sensitivity to the beautiful and joyful. On the other hand, some resilient folks retain a remarkable capacity to find satisfactions and joys regardless of the hardships that beset them. An example of this is found in one of the Balkan countries—Bulgaria, I believe—where people find joy in giving gifts. No matter how poor, I'm told, they present flowers and other goodies to all visitors. In fact, if a visitor admires an object in the house, it may be pressed upon him as a gift.

True wealth is the ability to find happiness in the simple, unexpected, or predictable surprises of every day. The only way to bequeath such an inheritance to one's children is by example. The father or mother who finds delight in reading stories, looking at the stars, marveling over a spider's web, writing letters, and talking with friends passes along a priceless way of living, a treasure no one can ever lose.

Children learn to enjoy whatever brightens their parent's countenance. If only a new Lexus will put a spark in Dad's eye, the children are not likely to be inspired by a hummingbird. If Mom's blues lift only after a bountiful shopping spree, her model carves itself into the children's psyche. When father and mother derive gratification only from hard work and clean floors, bike rides and table games are not likely to be the inheritance of their children.

Blessed may be those who can have it all—dependable cars, comfortable homes, and also an eye, ear, and palate for the simple treasures that satisfy and enrich. The truly well-off are those who, whether financially rich or poor, have inherited the earth. Envying no one, "the cockles of their hearts" are quickly warmed by everyday, hour-to-hour, garden-variety joys. They also know whom to thank.

SCRIPTURE REFLECTIONS

PSALM 89:15-17

Happy are the people who know the festal shout,
who walk, O LORD, in the light of your countenance;
they exult in your name all day long,
and extol your righteousness.
For you are the glory of their strength. . . .

What are some of the thoughts and emotions of those who are aware of the presence of God in their lives?

PSALM 92:13-15

They are planted in the house of the LORD;
they flourish in the courts of our God.
In old age they still produce fruit;
they are always green and full of sap,
showing that the LORD is upright;
he is my rock, and there is no unrighteousness in him.

"What is my only comfort in life and in death?" Answer this well-known catechism question in your own words.

PERSONAL REFLECTION

1. What makes some people able to remain joyful regardless of hardships that may beset them?

2. Are you that kind of person? If so, how do you maintain your joy in hardships?

   If not, how do you see your problem? If sometimes, where do you need to make change?

3. What "wealth" have you observed in your world recently? If you need focus, list several places you can look. What did you find?

4. Set a clock for 15 minutes. Do this work outside, either in early morning or late (dark) evening. Working as fast as you can, list all the "garden-variety" joys you see around you.

   How do you feel?

8

GIVING BIRTH DOES NOT MAKE A MOTHER

othering and fathering is not about baby-making. It is about person-molding and spirit-building.

A young woman who was adopted when she was three years old recently made arrangements to meet with her "real mother." They met. They talked. But the young woman quickly realized that she had been mistaken: this woman was not her real mother. Yes, this was the woman in whom she had been conceived and with whom she had spent her first three years. But her real mother was the one who had cared for her, nurtured and loved her, worked, struggled, agonized, and played with her all the years of her growing up. Mothering, properly understood, is spiritual care—person-building, not baby-making.

A bystander once called out to Jesus, "Blessed is the mother who gave you birth and nursed you." Jesus volleyed back to her: "Blessed rather are those who hear the word of God and obey it." Jesus' reply points out that there is nothing particularly significant about giving birth, even if the offspring turns out to be phenomenally successful. What really counts is what kind of person you are, what the condition of your heart is, how you are directed spiritually.

Another time Jesus revealed the same outlook. He was speaking to an audience when someone ran up and told him his mother and brothers were looking for him. Unfazed, he retorted: "Who is my mother, and who are my brothers . . . ? Whoever does the will of my Father in heaven is my brother and sister and mother."

In other words, some relationships are more important than blood and genetic kinship, more important even than our ties with the loving parents who raised us. Eventually we will draw the growing, maturing, and strengthening we need from a larger family—a spiritual family. Parents may advise, help, care for, critique, and offer very wonderful, practical, appreciated benefits, but the child must move on to other sources for the next stages of growth.

The time comes when we as parents must give our children up. The next generation needs to find new sources for continued maturation. Carefully nurtured and prepared at home, they must be launched into a new world, boosted on by fresh forces and sources, a new family of friends, loved ones, colleagues.

Jesus' words described what Mary and the others needed to realize about him. As he embarked on his ministry, he had to tune his heart and mind into other people. Never dishonoring his mother, he indicated that it was time to revise their relationship. He had to move on. She needed to let go and adjust to this new phase of his life and hers.

This experience is ours too. Though our family of nurture retains its specialness, we discover others who are vital to our growth. These new ones are those who share our pilgrimage. They are those struggling in similar arenas, trying to do the Lord's will in the same marketplace. These are the new mothers and sisters and brothers for whom we care in a deep and special way.

What a shock! To lose our children to other people—strangers often. To experience them forming allegiances to friends, colleagues, spouses—allegiances that are strong, deep, and equal or even higher in priority than theirs to us.

But this is the goal of parenting—to give our children away, to let them go, to send them on to others while we continue to support, as needed, prayerfully and carefully, from a little farther back, behind the lines.

Another event involving Jesus and his mother took place at the cross. Mary was there with her son's best friend, John. Jesus said to her, "Take John as your son." To John he said, "Take my mother to be your mother."

How free and flexible Jesus was with the idea of family. He could easily give his mother to a friend. At rock bottom he saw the essence of motherhood in the caring concern, the selfless relationship of one to another. He knew his mother's love and paid her the supreme compliment when arranging this new relationship. He knew she could include John. He knew she could be a mother to him. Flesh and blood were not the main things. Love can bring new people into one's circle.

Jesus continually taught that a good person is not defined by external markings, genetics, or position. And in this case he is qualifying what a mother is. Historically a mother is the source of love, kindness, comfort, security, compassion. She teaches, guides, inspires. She sees to it that what is needed is provided. As we grow up, we find these qualities in others—teachers, friends, aunts, neighbors, sisters, nurses—and sometimes in those who have never born a child physically.

As a Christian community we should be a whole network of fathers and mothers who can create an umbrella of care, guidance, correction, and every other form of love over each individual. Then the community can adjust and the family can shift a little to cover the vulnerable ones.

There is no special virtue in being the physical source of a baby. But there is virtue in embodying the qualities needed to enhance, facilitate, and enable another person to grow and become what God intended him or her to be. So physical mothers or fathers may be no parents at all. Or they may be the best. Whatever the case, a lot of people other than the birth parents may be doing the real fathering and mothering. God honors them. We should too.

SCRIPTURE REFLECTIONS

1 SAMUEL 1:26-28

And she said, "Oh, my lord! As you live, my lord, I am the woman who was standing here in your presence, praying to the LORD. For this child I prayed, and the LORD has granted me the petition that I made to him. Therefore I have lent him to the LORD; as long as he lives, he is given to the LORD."

1. In a few words, summarize the wisdom you see in Hannah's statement to Eli.

2. How is she "revising" her relationship to her child?

3. Ultimately, to whom does every child belong?

4. What are some of the "parts" a parent plays in the life of a child?

Mothers: Fathers:

PERSONAL REFLECTIONS

1. List some of the ways children need to be helped to grow.

2. What part can some of the following people play?

Mother: _____

Father: _____

Adoptive parents: _____

Foster parents: _____

Aunts: _____

Uncles: _____

Cousins: _____

Grandparents: _____

Medical doctors: _____

Pastors: _____

Church schoolteachers

—Nursery: _____

—Preschool: _____

—Primary: _____

—Junior High: _____

—High School: _____

School teachers:_____

Neighbors: _____

Family friends: _____

3. What do you think it would have been like to have been Mary, Jesus' mother?

How and when do you think she began to "let go"?

4. What are some of the really hard parts of letting go of any child?

List some constructive actions that might make it easier.

9

THOSE WHO MESS US, BLESS US

Irritation and exasperation over chaos created by our offspring needs to be modulated by correct reassessment of what really matters in life.

The '67 Volkswagen bus in our driveway looked like a Brahma bull, head down, kicking up its rear legs. The vehicle's tail end was propped high on two heavy jack stands. Carefully gutted of its vital organs, it now bled large stains of oil on the concrete driveway. In the garage rested the motor, blocking any deserving cars from entering. The transmission was draining into two plastic garbage-can lids. The smell of ancient grease permeated the air.

I entered the house and nearly stumbled over a Gott lunch bucket and a large water bottle flung onto the foyer floor in the path of foot traffic.

In the den a big twenty-year-old man sprawled on the couch controlling the television. He announced that we would be watching the Olympics that night, and nothing else: "And don't touch it! It's programmed to record tonight's events." In the middle of the room were two grubby athletic shoes, dirty socks included, and an open book, *How to Keep Your VW Alive.*

"By the way, we're out of milk," the big one complained, "and what time is dinner?" We were then informed with a smile that he would be going out that evening and would like to use the newer of our two cars.

Our neat, controlled, empty-nest existence had been totally disrupted. The cars couldn't get into the garage. The driveway was a disgrace. Strange music dominated. The television and its room had been taken over. No longer could we come and go without forethought because of renewed concerns about borrowed cars and the disbursement of house keys.

Irritation and exasperation were welling up within me as I stomped past the grease and oil stains. My bad mood thickened as I kept running into the intruder's scattered stuff and then encountered the man himself reposing on our furniture.

I restrained myself. A caution light flashed in my brain. A warning pushed into my consciousness: "What will your life be like when there is no longer anyone to mess up your place and botch your plans?"

The question answered itself. A vision passed before my eyes. I saw the kind of environment I've fantasized about: Everything is neat and clean. A book I laid down in a certain place is still there a few days later. I can put my hands quickly on a crescent wrench because it is exactly where I left it. The food supply is predictable. The newspaper is intact. My CDs are in the machine; I only need to turn it on. I can watch educational television all I want. Beautiful! A life like that looks wonderful.

Maybe it was God who whispered "boring" in my ear. Suddenly my dream turned unpleasant. After boring came lonely.

My holler melted down to a few appropriate parental protests. The wind had gone out of my sails as I realized subliminally that he who messes us blesses us.

For years I've longed to be able to control my home environment, to be able to keep everything in its place. Now that the opportunity is near at hand, I'm tallying up the price. Order is purchased by moving people out. The cost is relationships. God's whisper says people first. Neatness second.

Right now I'm cherishing the temporary return of chaos. I am genuinely thanking God for this last gasp of ordinary family disorderliness. The ache to have everything neat and under control is clamoring loudly. But a clearer voice is rebuking me to value deeply the presence of this visitor, our youngest son, the mostly absent college student. He works hard, does his own wash, articulates strong values, has clear life goals. Clean driveways can wait.

Family life irreversibly drifts toward the final exodus of the younger generation. Until they exit, delicious upsetness reigns in the household.

God has gifted some folks with the capacity for hospitality. They adeptly juggle kids, house guests, and phone calls. Cluttered counters and stacked dishes do not ruffle them. They instinctively relish the richness in relationships. Their souls are revived by the footsteps of friends and the voices of children.

Others of us struggle. We long for deliverance into the promised land of peace and quiet. When these prayers are answered, however, we often ache for captivity again. Clean, empty space is appealing, but as a permanent condition it's spirit-sapping and depressing.

Christians are called into lives of personal relationships. When the kids pack, others must enter. Independent, antiseptic islands of isolation starve the soul.

I sympathize with young mothers and fathers as they frantically balance slim budgets and ravenous appetites. I empathize with them as they thirst for free time and are weary of constant demands, dirty dishes, and unfinished ironing. But in the middle of longing for release, yearning to move on to other personal goals, there ought to be an occasional cry of thanksgiving.

Life serves up little that can match the satisfaction, and irritations, of family activity. But children move away. Meanwhile our stern and frazzled ranting and raving over clutter and confusion ought to be tempered with a twinkle of joy.

SCRIPTURE REFLECTIONS

PSALM 127:3-5

Lo, children are a heritage of the LORD: and the fruit of the womb is his reward. As arrows are in the hand of a mighty man; so are children of the youth. Happy is the man that hath his quiver full of them (KJV).

Describe some of the ways that children bring us happiness.

EPHESIANS 6:4

And, fathers, do not provoke your children to anger, but bring them up in the discipline and instruction of the Lord.

What is the difference between discipline, instruction, and the kind of iron rules that sap the spirit?

Give examples:

Discipline	Instruction	"Spirit-sapping"
_____	_____	_____
_____	_____	_____
_____	_____	_____
_____	_____	_____
_____	_____	_____

COLOSSIANS 3:21

Fathers, do not provoke your children, or they may lose heart.

1. How would you encourage a six-year-old?

2. If you were twelve, what would you perceive as parental discouragement?

3. How would you encourage a thirteen-year-old?

4. If you were sixteen, what would you perceive as parental discouragement?

PERSONAL REFLECTIONS

1. What blessings have you experienced from messy kids?

2. How do you encourage kids?

3. Which of your personality traits bring you in conflict with the messiness of kids?

4. If you were being judged by a child, what would your actions say? (Circle one in each set.)

You like older or younger children best.

You would rather do sticker books or clean rooms.

You would rather plant flowers or gather trash.

You would rather read books at home or go to the library.

You would rather cook or clean the kitchen.

You would rather sit at the dinner table or get the dishes done.

You would rather throw Frisbees or give the dog a bath.

5. Do any of your actions and reactions to kids need improvement? For each item, give yourself an S (satisfactory) or an N (needs improvement).

___ Your focus is on kids' needs rather than home orderliness.

___ You pay more attention to your TV program than to kids.

___ You become angry when children raise their voices in play.

___ You become angry when children raise their voices in anger.

___ Helping with homework is a peaceful, learning time.

___ You enjoy your children's presence in the room with you.

___ You are frustrated by fingerprints on the coffee table.

___ You talk easily with kids in general.

___ You talk easily with your own kids.

___ You feel time pressure when you try to spend quality time with kids.

10

ENCOURAGE EACH OTHER

Empty your mind of all the positive thoughts stored there, doing no one any good. A daily inventory of anybody's thought bank turns up stacks and stacks of unspoken kind words, warm feelings held back, and grateful impulses reserved.

People need these goods. Soul food must be passed around, not warehoused in our hearts as so many warm feelings.

A tide of blessing could sweep our world if millions of encouragement doors swung open. It would wash away a lot of hurt and spread like wildflowers.

F red Vetch was sixty-seven years old when his father died. The two men had worked side by side for forty-nine years in the mill their family had owned for several generations.

When Fred nervously took over the mill after his father's death, he realized he could not recall receiving, in all those years together, a compliment from his father. Not a pat on the back, not an "atta boy," not a word of praise had passed his father's lips. Criticisms, complaints, and scoldings were sprinkled throughout his life, but Fred had never received a word of direct encouragement. No clear, unmistakable message of approval, never a "Well done, son" slipped quietly into his paycheck or his heart.

This strange reality had dawned on him originally some years earlier. A friend had commented over coffee that Fred's dad must be awfully pleased to have Fred around to take over the mill. The friend surmised that the father must be proud of how Fred was building up the business. The remark did not slide lightly past Fred. He pondered it for several minutes that morning. Then he answered, "I don't know if he is pleased or proud or what. He has never said anything about it. I assume he is, but, frankly, I don't know."

Fred is not alone. There are many men and women in their thirties, forties, and fifties today, some with parents close at hand, who have never received an encouraging word from their father or mother. These are not folks from illiterate, ignorant families. They grew up in intelligent, educated, well-off environments. They are from homes they appreciate and stay in touch with. As adult children, they honor, respect, and love their parents. And they know their parents feel the same toward them. *But no one ever says so.*

Fathers seem stingier than mothers when it comes to giving verbal support. More than once I have heard young men and women exclaim about their father's tears of apparent pride at their graduation—after which they heard not one "I'm so proud of you, honey" or "Good work, son."

Stories are not scarce, either, of sons and daughters happily returning home with great news of a new job or promotion and having Dad ask, "What does it pay?"—instead of giving his child a hearty hug of congratulations for the accomplishment.

Those who grow up deprived of encouraging words are most likely to repeat that behavior toward their own children. Having heard few compliments ourselves, we may not find it natural or comfortable to pay a direct compliment, to say words of praise face-to-face. Praise and compliments bring a level of intimacy that for some is scary territory to enter. Others just do not think of doing it.

Praising others is a highly desirable, beautiful, and constructive habit to cultivate. God wants us to build each other up as best we can. Compliments, words of appreciation, pats on the back, and notes of praise make solid and unforgettable marks on the people to whom we give them. These deeds lift spirits. They make people feel better. And when we feel better, we do better. We become more productive builders of the kingdom of Christ.

So we need to learn to speak our minds. It's easy to overlook the attributes and positive qualities of those to whom we are closest. We silently appreciate them but take them for granted. We need to step back and think about each of the people near and dear to us. Ten seconds of reflection will highlight their obviously praiseworthy traits, attitudes, or accomplishments. Then say something!

"Eric, I really appreciate your cheerfulness at breakfast every morning."

"Pam, I sure admire the way you support your friends."

"Cal, your musical ability has brought us so much joy over the years."

"Milly, I like the way you answer the telephone."

"Mark, your sense of humor really tickles me."

Encouraging words do not just enter the ear and travel into a recording space in the brain. They are far more potent than that. They enter the ear, are processed by the brain, and travel into the cells, electrons, and atoms of the whole body. The chemistry of the entire person is affected by words. Encouraging words are spirit-lifting and physically energizing. The human brain works like a pharmacy. Good words trigger positive medicines.

The apostle Paul tells us through his writings to the early church that encouraging each other is a high priority. It isn't good enough that Fred Vetch had to assume that his father appreciated him. His soul thirsted for the lasting benefits of a specific blessing—words of support, encouragement, and gratitude.

Fred's father's reservoir of appreciation failed to overflow on his son. But fathers aren't the only ones who need to spill praise and encouragement. We all store blessings we can bestow. Good words build each other up.

SCRIPTURE REFLECTIONS

JUDE 1

1:3 "Beloved . . ."

1:17 "But you, beloved . . ."

1:20 "But you, beloved . . ."

1:24 "Now to him who is able to keep you from falling, and to make you stand without blemish . . ."

1. In this letter, we find stern warning and correction. How does the word "beloved" make correction easier to hear?

2. How does encouragement, such as "and to make you stand without blemish," make correction easier to hear?

MATTHEW 25:23

His master said to him, "Well done, good and trustworthy slave; you have been trustworthy in a few things, I will put you in charge of many things; enter into the joy of your master."

1. Why do we so often neglect the words "Well done"?

2. What prevents us from expressing our "joy" to and with others?

3. What first steps can we take toward change in this area?

PERSONAL REFLECTIONS

1. **Rate yourself (N=needs improvement, S=satisfactory, E=excellent):**

   Are you a person of many loving words? ___

   Are you able to express your feelings? ___

   Are you able to express your joy? ___

   Do you compliment people often? ___

   Do you "think" more compliments than you give? ___

   Do you often wish you could find words to express your thoughts? ___

   Can you express yourself by touching? ___

   Do you give as many hugs as you feel inside? ___

   Do you keep your hugs in your thoughts? ___

   Are you better at "wishing you could" than expressing yourself? ___

   Are your ratings where you would like them to be? ___

2. Plan and give three compliments.

3. Plan and express words of appreciation to three people.

4. Plan to and pat the backs of three people.

5. Write three notes of praise.

11

THERE ARE GOOD REASONS FOR A KID'S BEHAVIOR

*C*hildren can do dumb things for very good reasons. Respectful love builds bridges of friendship that endure for generations.

When his mother noticed Steve and his young friend making hurried trips to the outside water faucet with their little bucket, she investigated. Coming out of the house, she immediately smelled smoke. Rushing to the front, she found vigorously burning leaves already scorching the wooden siding of the house. The preschoolers' frantic efforts to extinguish the spreading blaze were not working, but she was able quickly to put it out.

Steve, still sobbing in terror from the losing fight they'd been waging, readily admitted starting the fire.

"Why would you do such a thing?" his nearly hysterical mother demanded.

"Because Smokey the Bear said, 'You should light a fire when the wind isn't blowing.' And you told me today the wind isn't blowing," he explained, puzzled that a flaw could be hidden in this logic.

Then Linda remembered that earlier that day he had wanted to go to the park and fly his kite. She had told him there was no breeze. They had to wait for a windy day.

She also recalled having read the little guy a "Smokey the Bear" story in which Smokey admonished his readers, "Never light a fire on a windy day. Always light a fire on a day when there is no wind."

And that's what he did! His actions were perfectly reasonable to him: "No wind. Time to light a fire."

Another time, in the same year, Steve went to visit his friend Kent. Some hours later, Kent's mother brought Steve home kicking and screaming. Totally mystified, she reported that he absolutely did not want to come home.

Eventually he calmed down, and the pieces of the story came together: One day in mid-November Steve had been at Kent's house, playing outside. He had with him a miniature toy cannon. Sometime during the day it began to snow very heavily, and the cannon got covered and lost. Very upset, he was reassured they would recover it when the snow melted. Today was three months later. The ground was still covered with three feet of snow, but the temperature was 35 degrees. *The snow was melting!* And Steve was waiting.

So his behavior was logical. He wasn't, as it appeared, being stubborn, balky, defiant, and naughty. "You said I could get my cannon when the snow melted, and it was melting today," he explained. He planned to stay right there until the lost toy came into sight. A sensible idea, but he lacked the information that the thawing would probably take at least another forty-eight hours.

If adults were clever enough to understand, we would discover that much of what our littlest ones do that irritates, aggravates, or upsets us are valid uproars. Something in their system is being frustrated, and they are trying to get it changed.

We must respect our children—at all ages. Even newborn cries are to be respected as meaningful behavior, not seen as the noise of naughtiness or random outbursts of a malfunctioning mechanism.

The word "respect" literally means to look back at. That implies the opposite of overlooking, disregarding, ignoring. It contains the idea of taking a second look to see what is really there and taking it seriously.

In beginning a relationship with a new baby, we start on the right foot when we consciously see this fresh creation of God as a wondrous mystery whose language we are challenged to understand as we endeavor to facilitate his or her blossoming.

That is only the beginning. Parents who respect their infants will establish a pattern of lifelong openness to them. Such relationships eventually can yield the wonderful reward of friendship with one's adult children, the proper goal of all nurturing.

A boring speaker once woke me to full alertness with the matter-of-fact observation that "children are probably closer to God than grown-ups are." That statement struck me because it was so obviously true while being universally overlooked. Jesus said, "Unless you become like little children, you will never enter the kingdom of heaven."

Children need the security of parents who are in control. Parents who do their job best manage the driver's seat with an eye and ear delicately tuned to the wisdom and insights of youth and the logic in the fires they start.

SCRIPTURE REFLECTIONS

PROVERBS 22:6

Train children in the right way,
and when old, they will not stray.

What "how to's" might you give a parent for training a child in the right way?

EPHESIANS 6:4

And, fathers, do not provoke your children to anger, but bring them up in the discipline and instruction of the Lord.

1. Do parents sometimes "provoke" their children? Give several examples:

2. What situations might provoke a child and should be avoided?

3. What are some of the problems in the following:

Playing too rough_____

Play hitting_____

Teasing_____

Joking_____

Name-calling_____

Scare tactics_____

Hiding_____

Lying_____

PERSONAL REFLECTIONS

1. Name some positive ways of dealing with

naughtiness:

crankiness:

tantrums:

2. How can you show respect for

a baby?

a two-year-old?

an eight-year-old?

a teenager?

an adult child?

3. What are several qualities of parents who are in control?

4. What are several qualities of a parent who is not in control?

5. Do you have any special ways of dealing with children? If you are in a small group, share your nuggets.

12

FLYING THROUGH ADOLESCENCE

*T*radition calls us to give two vital necessities to our children: "roots" and "wings." When we translate "roots" and "wings" into practical wisdom, we come up with the difficult challenge of holding on while letting go. That challenge is especially daunting for parents of adolescents, who are often called on to perform a balancing act sorely in need of divine guidance. Humility, trust, and steady prayer help create the environment youth need to stay connected while stretching forward to occupy new territories to which God calls them.

*C*ommunicate is not the right word for interactions between teenagers and their parents. What you do with teenagers is try to *stay in touch*.

Communication implies a mutual interest base, something that doesn't exist between parents and teenagers. Parents want it. Teens are busy with something else.

The primary (and appropriate) drive in teenagers' lives at this age is toward approval by peers, not parents. Teens have a need for parental approval, but you can't see it through their thick facade of indifference and even, sometimes, defiance.

We can give our children two precious gifts modeled on our Creator's relationship with us: roots and wings. By rooting them early in deep, resilient spirituality and emotional flexibility, we prepare them for life's inevitable storms and droughts, as well as for times of plenty. And after doing that, we have to give them wings. *Now it is their time to fly.*

Christ's parable of the prodigal son contains this enormously important and often overlooked lesson: the father is able to let the son go. This is how our Father in heaven has treated us from the dawn of creation. He invites us into relationship with him, but he does not coerce or manipulate us. He gives us abundant permission to roam, but also sets boundaries beyond which humanity must not go.

So it should be with teenagers. They must have plenty of room to fly—to try their wings in new relationships, to be independent (or at least to enjoy the illusion of independence), to explore the world of work and adventure—with limits set and known.

Perhaps the greatest challenge for parents of teens is giving up the need to control. Parents who hang onto control set the stage for intense power struggles that either parent or child may win. If the parent "wins," the child's rebellion may go underground. He will express independence by doing his own thing out of sight of home, or sometimes will postpone it until later years. If the child "wins," she loses the security of having a person stronger than she is. She then becomes the center of her universe—which is a terrifying prospect and the mother of misconduct as well.

Neither party must win. They must stay in touch and constantly negotiate. Living with teenagers is an art. Some of the following specific suggestions can help make it work:

1. Make Time.

The importance of just being with your teenagers cannot be over-rated. The concept of "quality time" is questionable at this stage. Ten rides to school together in silence may yield one meaningful verbal interchange. Quantity of time begets quality of relationship. A dozen family dinners communicate a cafeteria-load of love and security.

2. Trust Them.

Blind trust is naive and dangerous. But lack of trust is disastrous. It may be better to err on the side of trust than to err toward suspicion.

Part of trust is suspending the need to know what is going on in a teenager's life. Let there be ample acres of "private property."

Most of what we need to know is readily observable: grades, health, attitudes, friends, study habits, entertainment tastes, nourishment, values.

We do not need to know exactly where he went after last night's game and what he had to eat or what her friends are doing about the upcoming party. It's fine to ask. But graciously observe the "No Trespassing" signs.

3. Allow for Minor Deviance!

Parents ought not to like everything about their teenage children. So it's probably wise to tolerate originality and weirdness in truly unimportant things like clothes and hairstyles. Save the artillery for the crucial battles.

Deviation is the way identity-seeking youth go about becoming persons separate from their parents, even though their deviance may actually be in lock-step conformity with their peers. By allowing teens to demonstrate their independence in fringe matters, parents may prevent major departures from important spiritual and moral values.

4. Exploit Common Interests.

If she likes to shop, seize every opportunity to join her. If she likes sports, read the sports news and talk with her about it. Watch TV with him, even if you have to yield to his choice. Initiate special outings that tie into his known passions—skiing, for example.

5. Purge Your Hopes and Aspirations.

It is natural to get vicarious satisfaction through the accomplishments of the part of yourself that is your son or daughter. Overinvestment in our children's success, however, sets up for disappointment and puts undue pressure on them.

Christian parents should have high hopes and aspirations for their children. First among these hopes, it seems, should be that their offspring develop healthy relationships. Hard work, financial success, obedience, popularity, fame, and prestige are worth little compared to the capacity to have meaningful, fulfilling relationships with God, people, and nature. And positive ability to connect well with others is a major key to all success.

6. Pray!

Praying one-on-one with teenagers may create more intimacy and piety than they can bear. Forcing it may do more to turn a teenager away from the faith than toward it. Model for their future practice, allowing them to mature at their own speed.

Still, mentioning your teenager's name in mealtime prayers is spirit-nourishing. Teenagers get deep support from hearing, in casual situations, that you remember them in prayer—even though they rarely acknowledge it and may grimace with embarrassment at the moment.

7. Praise and Encourage Them.

Warnings and admonitions flow automatically and abundantly from parents' mouths. So parents need to also deliberately and intentionally turn on praise and encouragement. And they need to do so even when they don't feel like it. Praise is what teenagers need.

Parents need to regularly broadcast heartwarming words like, "You really look nice this morning," even though they don't get an appreciative response from the targeted one.

As in gardening, so also in teen-rearing: great joys come from a well-tended crop. But the raising of God's special creatures is far more delicate and mysterious than the raising of fruits and flowers. With patience, prayer, and trust in God's promises, we each do our best, aided by the support of caring communities. The single most important ingredient for fruitful crops is good soil. The home is the soil; when properly balanced, good results are guaranteed.

SCRIPTURE REFLECTIONS

GENESIS 1:28

God blessed them, and God said to them, "Be fruitful and multiply, and fill the earth and subdue it; and have dominion over the fish of the sea and over the birds of the air and over every living thing that moves upon the earth."

If God knew that human beings would destroy and pollute the earth, why do you think God gave us the power of dominion?

LUKE 15:12

The younger of them said to his father, "Father, give me the share of the property that will belong to me." So he divided his property between them.

1. Why was it necessary for the father to let the younger son go?

2. Why do we want to hold on to our children's lives?

3. Why do we need to let go at the appropriate time?

4. Why is that often so hard to do?

PERSONAL REFLECTIONS

1. **How do you spend quality time with your**

   children?

   friends?

   family?

2. **In what ways are you accepting of teens? Adults?**

3. **What are your common interests with teens?**

4. **If you have children, in what ways are your hopes and aspirations for them realistic? Unrealistic?**

5. **Suggest some good ways to include teens in prayer times.**

6. **Are you an encourager? Give examples.**

13

LAUGHTER AND OTHER SPIRIT-BOOSTING VITAMINS

God gives us good reasons to laugh.

F inally we settled on the suitcase we wanted to buy and found our way to the checkout. Linda signed the charge slip, then inquired about where we needed to go to pick up the merchandise. It was that kind of store.

The harried and hurried cashier answered indifferently, hastily mumbling the directions to the loading dock: "Three lef's 'round the building to door number 3."

Linda, a careful person, slowly and clearly repeated back to the clerk what she thought she had heard: "Okay, three laps around the building to door number 3."

"Three lefts! Not three laps," the awakened clerk corrected.

Too late. The hilarious mental picture of us having to jog three laps around the giant department store before they'd give us the suitcase had doubled me over with laughter. Then Linda caught it. Out of control, with tears running down our faces, we laughed our way around the building to the merchandise dock.

As we drove about for the rest of our errands that morning, every little while one of us would begin to chuckle. One chuckle plunged us right back into full-scale laughter for another five minutes. We felt fantastic that day. Chuckles, chortles, and giggles kept melting our tensions away.

Nearly five decades ago *Reader's Digest* claimed that laughter is the best medicine. More recently several very convincing stories have again testified to the strong role of laughter in the healing process. Norman Cousins credited laughing over Allan Funt's *Candid Camera* shows for boosting him to victory over a believed incurable disease.

Today we understand God's miraculous creation of the human person more than ever. The physical body far surpasses mere machines. Think of yourself as an intricate spiritual and physical organism needing careful vigilance to maintain a healthy balance. Abuse of the body by heavy consumption of fats and cholesterol-laden foods can kill it. So will chronic ingestion of cigarette smoke into the lungs. In the same way, conditions that hammer the spirit, like grief and loneliness, take a harsh toll on immunity. Noxious circumstances, like bad food and dirty air, sicken and weaken us.

Spirit-lifting activities, such as laughter, actually produce measurable positive biochemical changes in the body. Obviously laughter generates pleasant feelings, but the effects last longer than the moment and spread the good beyond the buoyancy of spirit or the mind. Measurable physical changes also follow. The whole body reverberates with well-being. Cells sing. Tissues celebrate. Organs dance. Health soars.

Bible writers knew all this. Proverbs says, "A cheerful heart is a good medicine." Ancient wisdom preached and practiced the essential connection between an elevated spirit and good health, a happy soul and efficient digestion.

In the medical world a variety of soul-soothing, body-enhancing, spirit-caressing activities are creeping into the treatment of the ill. They include touch, humor, music, videos of beautiful sounds and scenery, improving the ambiance and colors of the hospital room, prayer, and meditation. These additions also aid marketing, but their real purpose is making people well.

One experiment in the orthopedic surgery department of a major hospital found that patients visited by the chaplain before an opera-tion recovered better. Those called on received information about what to expect and were ministered to with prayer and pastoral care. This group moved on more quickly, ingested less pain-killing medication, and went home sooner. Information and care fortified them, lessened their anxiety, jacked up their confidence, and enabled their bodies to bounce back speedily.

Dispiriting conditions like discouragement, fear, worry, guilt, anxiety, grief, and excessive pressure sicken and weaken us just like too much fat or cholesterol. Unfortunately every Christian home lives with many of these toxins. They are a natural and inevitable part of life as we know it. But we do know how to neutralize some of them, and intentional efforts to do so in the home pay blessed dividends. Spirit-lifting antidotes such as good humor, laughter, and cheering words wash away the poisons frequently infecting our souls. Beauty, encouragement, the listening ear, acceptance, touch, and soul-soothing music help. Flowers, family outings and games, quiet times, and love all heal. Vacations and hobbies must season our days to refresh our souls. Appropriately sprinkled into our family routines, these potent spiritual "antibiotics" kill the germs of gloom, bitterness, fear, stress, and the other enemies within and around that tear down our vitality.

Above and beyond all these wonderful healers is the therapeutic joy of hope. Laughter eventually rings hollow without a solution to the big questions of life—questions like "Who am I?", "What is life about?", and "How can I face death?" Christian faith proclaims the true basis for ultimate cheer, deep laughter, and inspiration without limits. Whole-person health flourishes when we know who we belong to and that what we do matters. Equipped for living by God's truth and with Christ's presence, we break free to be tickled by all God's eye-opening, heart-warming, and metabolism-enhancing gifts. Then we—both as individuals and families—can really laugh and enjoy full health.

SCRIPTURE REFLECTIONS

PROVERBS 17:22

A cheerful heart is a good medicine, but a downcast spirit dries up the bones.

1. **Describe the characteristics of a person you know who radiates a cheerful heart.**

2. **What, in your opinion, is the source of his or her cheerfulness?**

PSALM 103:1-5

Bless the LORD, O my soul,
and all that is within me,
bless his holy name.
Bless the LORD, O my soul,
and do not forget all his benefits—
who forgives all your iniquity,
who heals all your diseases,
who redeems your life from the Pit,
who crowns you with steadfast love and mercy,
who satisfies you with good as long as you live
so that your youth is renewed like the eagle's.

Read the passage through several times. Then close your eyes and meditate on what you have just read.

1. List several of God's benefits to you and to your family.

2. List several things for which God has forgiven you.

3. Review several times you or someone in your family has been healed.

4. Review the times you and members of your family have been well.

5. Review God's steadfast love and mercy in your life and the life of your family.

How are you feeling?

PERSONAL REFLECTIONS

1. What spirit-lifting antidotes have you tried in your home?

What new ones might you try?

2. During the course of this study

Watch a funny movie or video either alone or with other members of your family. Describe how you feel afterwards.

Go to a park and watch children at play. What did you observe?

Spend a half hour watching a pet. Did you learn anything? What?

Spend some time, either alone or with your family, listening to your favorite music. What effect did it have on you?

Find a garden of flowers. List your observations.

Share some time with a friend or with a member of your family. How do you feel?

Tell a joke.

3. Are you healthy? Would a merry heart improve your health or lifestyle? List some ways in which you can bring this positive change into your life and your family life.

14

TOUCH HEALS MORE THAN SKIN-DEEP

T ouch, physical contact, skin-to-skin, blesses, heals, reassures, comforts.

The radiant young couple trembled, teared, and choked with emotion as they promised their commitments and spoke their vows. They locked fingers as I laid my hand on theirs and pronounced them husband and wife. As rehearsed, they then kneeled for the prayer. Side by side they carefully assumed the traditional posture, their hands now separated, each grasping the kneeling bench rail independently. I whispered for them to join their hands, and they did.

Nearly every time I officiate at a wedding this little drama repeats itself. Each loving twosome resonates with strong physical affinity for each other; then they pull apart for the prayer.

When I think of it in advance, at premarital sessions, I coach prospective wedders on this detail. But the idea goes beyond the ceremony. I recommend to them that they hold hands every time they bow their heads in prayer, wherever it may be—mealtime at home, in restaurants, in church services—for the rest of their lives. This simple childlike linkage is not only a pleasant bonding agent but also is a strong symbolic act of unity.

Hand-holding at table grace has become a ritual in our family in recent years. Once initiated, lack of physical connection during prayer feels odd and wrong, like something vital is missing. Our new tradition is not yet enthusiastically embraced by the young adult males. Touching each other, or holding a parent's hand, obviously still provokes squeamishness of some Neanderthal origin. But our sons do wholeheartedly accept and return the warm hugs of greeting and farewell, now a nonnegotiable part of our family life.

The importance of flesh-to-flesh contact is not a recent discovery, but its value is more clearly understood today. Our skin has been called the largest organ of the body and its stimulation an enhancer of emotional, physical, and spiritual health.

One of the major infirmities in the life of nursing home residents is skin hunger. Nobody lays a reassuring or caressing hand on many disabled or forgotten elderly people. This neglect substantially contributes to the general debilitation of people of all ages. Touch brings life.

It is legendary that untouched, unheld babies fail to thrive and die. Rapidly becoming a lighthearted legend is the claim that the greatest cure-all for life's ailments is a heavy, daily dose of human hugs. And there may be enough truth in this legend to inspire personal practice. Friendly, sociable embracing and touching is virgin territory for many, especially males. I know that's true for me. I haven't been resisting with kicking and screaming as hugging becomes a daily form of greeting and parting among the company I keep. But for me, practicing physical contact requires a decisive overriding of a strong congenital, or learned, inner reserve. Gradually this warmer way feels like the natural and right thing to do. To just shake hands now feels cold, distant, standoffish.

There is good biblical precedence for more emphasis on the physical. The role of touch was prominent in Jesus' ministry. Often his healing acts included some form of physical contact. The same is true of the apostles, who laid hands on and healed the people to whom they ministered. James's prescription for the sick includes the touch of hands anointing the body with oil. Likewise, Paul calls for greeting each other with a holy kiss, another warm physical action that even ardent scriptural literalists ignore for some reason.

Sick and injured people commonly quickly regress to honest and open childlike vulnerability, expressed clearly through their response to an offer of prayer. All eagerly accept! But something else regularly happens as I stand bedside with head bowed. One hundred percent of those I visit—without cue, prompting, or leading—reach out a hand to be held. It's like they went to school and learned the protocol for patient life. Old people or young, male or female, macho or wimp, want to connect "five." Often, when it feels appropriate, I add a lightly placed hand to their forehead and speak words of blessing. This too is conspicuously appreciated. Usually I am awarded the gift of a tear or two trickling down a cheek.

Therapeutic touch is carefully taught today in schools of nursing. Measurable changes in heartbeat, hemoglobin levels, blood pressure, and other health indicators are observable when the patient is intentionally and skillfully touched by nursing staff.

Years ago in a cardiac research program, a technician noticed that on the electrocardiogram printout periodic islands of normal heartbeat showed up in the midst of the badly damaged rhythms. Keen sleuth work soon pinpointed the origin of these healthy moments. They occurred when the nurses touched and cared for the patient. Severely broken hearts were temporarily healed by the necessary touch of medical care.

A share of this business is snidely put down as "touchy-feely" stuff by intellectuals, those who think they live mostly in their heads. Others who squirm and sweat over tactile interaction will find their own escape routes from this kind of intimacy.

But modern discoveries now verify what many have known intuitively. Spiritual leaders have always laid hands on the sick and afflicted to tap into the health force residing in physical touch. Healing flows mysteriously, but effectively, out of the hearts and minds of pastors, parents, partners, and friends. Through their outstretched fingers, healing streams into the afflicted, renewing, refreshing, reviving.

SCRIPTURE REFLECTIONS

1 CORINTHIANS 16:20

All the brothers and sisters send greetings. Greet one another with a holy kiss.

LUKE 15:20

So he set off and went to his father. But while he was still far off, his father saw him and was filled with compassion; he ran and put his arms around him and kissed him.

1. **What are some emotions you feel when you read the above Scriptures?**

2. **Rate your reactions to touch on a scale from 1-5 (1=very positive, 5=very negative):**

   I like it when my parents hug each other. ____

   I like it when my parents hug me. ____

   I find it hard to hug spontaneously. ____

   I am comfortable when children hug me. ____

   I am comfortable when my friends embrace me. ____

   I would embrace someone who was crying. ____

   I like to hold hands with

       parents. ____

       friends of the same sex. ____

       husband or wife. ____

       my children. ____

       little children. ____

       teenagers. ____

PERSONAL REFLECTIONS

1. List some situations in which you might use touch to express feelings. What kind of touch would you use in each situation?

2. List several forms of "healing" touch.

3. Why do you think touch becomes easier as a person gets older?

4. During this study, try the following once and relate your feelings.

Kiss a friend on the cheek. _____

Hug someone of the same sex. _____

Embrace your mother. _____

Embrace your father. _____

Embrace a sister or brother. _____

Softly lay your hand on someone's cheek. _____

Hold a small child on your lap. _____

Shake hands with a child. _____

Hold hands with a friend. _____

Sit on someone's lap. _____

Have someone sit on your lap. _____

Wrestle in fun with someone. _____

Play with a pet in the grass. _____

5. What are your favorite ways to express feelings?

15

INTIMIDATION GETS GOOD RESULTS— IMMEDIATELY

What does it take to move you to action? If you respond best to threats and intimidation and slowly to suggestions, hints, and needs, some spiritual revision is needed.

During the record heat of July, the massive central air conditioner for our fourteen-story office building failed. The windows of this modern structure do not open, so by 9 a.m. my east-exposure study was like a sauna, and the rest of the offices only slightly less hot.

The repair people came to fix the system, but there were no immediate results. Days passed. A week went by. Cordially each of us inquired about the progress and urged haste. Patiently we endured a second week, keeping a good-humored attitude most of the time. But in the middle of the fourth week of enduring stifling temperatures, our business manager hit the ceiling. He raged at the air-conditioning experts who were supposedly fixing the problem. And suddenly things changed. They began taking shorter lunch breaks and arriving promptly in the morning. They told us they could install temporary portable devices. Very soon the sweltering tower was livable again.

Rage got results.

A few years ago we had new vinyl flooring installed in our kitchen. Shortly thereafter we also bought a new stove. In the process of bringing the appliance into the house, the workman badly cut the new flooring. Clearly visible, it was a major blemish. We called the appliance shop, asking for reparations or a solution of some kind. All efforts to achieve a satisfactory answer were met with delays, denials, and refusals. So I contacted an attorney. He wrote a strongly worded letter. The flooring was quickly repaired. Strong words are rewarded.

Legend has it that somewhere in the world there is a tribe with two gods. Each has its likeness prominently displayed in the villages. One is a kind god—patient, loving, and caring. The other is an angry god—vindictive, punitive, demanding. Although loyal subjects are expected to bring sacrifices to both, the angry god gets the majority of the gifts. Little is brought to the kind god. Appeasing the scary deity is crucial. Pleasing the long-suffering one is not regarded as urgent.

Menacing gets results. Hollering, swearing, and threatening moves people, motivates, gets jobs done, stimulates adrenaline flow. Scare people if you want them to work hard for you. There may still be schools of management where table-slapping and spleen-venting are taught as sure means of directing an organization into success.

It is a sad, but accurate, commentary on human behavior that scaring people is often an effective way to accomplish a task. However, anger and intimidation only pay off in the short run.

In the home, authoritarian parents who regiment their children by the use of General-Patton-style power tactics may see model behavior for a time. But scrutiny of the life course of their youth will usually show eventual rebellion, distancing, and rejection of the family values. Sometimes the next generation, lemming-like, repeats their parents' power techniques, with little apparent change and identical consequences.

It is important to teach children to be responsive to authority in respectful ways. So much of life includes needing to accept directions from those with seniority, expertise, and/or rank. Teenage work experience in grocery stores, fast-food outlets, or the military serves as a grueling training ground for one's capacity to take orders even from one's intellectual inferiors. The adult world, for most, requires submission to bosses. Those who cannot manage to submit are often among the homeless and unemployed.

Holding authority is different from being authoritarian. An authoritarian leader rules for the narrow purpose of getting a job done or maintaining personal control. He has little regard for the spirit or morale of the persons commanded. Such leadership ignores people and focuses on short-run production and orderliness. Such operations will not thrive long because of the dispiriting effect they have on human beings.

The threatening god gets all the gifts. But in the long run the angry god is also resented and despised. Every effort will be made to undermine his ruthless power. The frightening god receives abundant gratuities, but fear squelches and inhibits the confidence and creative development of his cowering subjects. Shriveled, spiritless people emerge from oppressive systems.

For building a strong family, business, or community, heavy-handedness fails in the long run. For a while insecure people (all of us) respond to the power approach. We may feel safe with a Vince Lombardi or Mike Ditka hollering orders at us with clinched fists. Such rock-like mannerisms cater to our own shakiness, tempting us to follow those who sound solidly confident. They send a counterfeit security into our souls.

But God has created us with an inner dignity that can only take so much bulldozing. Some souls are smashed early and live on that way, addicted to power. Others survive, rally to their own defense, and get away from such soul-killing influences—whether these be parents, preachers, or employers.

The air-conditioning repairmen and the appliance shop responded only when threatened. In many situations there seems to be no other way to get the job done. But resilient, productive communities, destined to last a long time, arise out of a different process. Organizations that value people share leadership. They listen to subordinates and struggle to refine a spirit-lifting methodology. Families and factories that discuss decisions and allow feelings and issues to be expressed show higher productivity over an extended time. Families, schools, shops, churches, offices, and every other grouping where Christians lead are also in the people-building business. That is what the Spirit of Christ does—builds people. Valuable products roll out of each organization established for a specific purpose, but all are God-ordained to care for the spirits of their people in the process. Such will be blessed.

SCRIPTURE REFLECTIONS

MARK 11:15-17

Then they came to Jerusalem. And he entered the temple and began to drive out those who were selling and those who were buying in the temple, and he overturned the tables of the money changers and the seats of those who sold doves; and he would not allow anyone to carry anything through the temple. He was teaching and saying, "Is it not written,

> *'My house shall be called a house of prayer for all the nations'? But you have made it a den of robbers."*

MATTHEW 17:1-2

Six days later, Jesus took with him Peter and James and his brother John and led them up a high mountain, by themselves. And he was transfigured before them, and his face shone like the sun, and his clothes became dazzling white.

JOHN 5:8 AND 14

Jesus said to him, "Stand up, take your mat and walk."

Later Jesus found him in the temple and said to him, "See, you have been made well! Do not sin anymore, so that nothing worse happens to you."

1. How do you explain Christ's cleansing of the temple? Why do you suppose it was needed?

2. How would you have felt if you were one of the disciples on the Mount of Transfiguration?

3. Describe your reaction to Jesus' gentleness in dealing with people.

How has he been gentle with you?

PERSONAL REFLECTIONS

1. List some short-term benefits of intimidation.

2. What makes us want to win by intimidation?

3. What do you see as the difference between authority and authoritarian?

   _____ vs. _____

   _____ vs. _____

   How can either or both be used to a productive end?

4. What are some of the characteristics of a person with inner dignity?

   How is it achieved?

5. How does the Spirit of Christ build people? How can you use that Spirit to build someone in your home?

16

LET'S GET SERIOUS ABOUT JOYFUL OCCASIONS

ard work, industriousness, and single-minded productivity bless the world enormously. Where would we be without them? But accomplishment without celebration, thanksgiving, and joyful noisemaking dries the soul.

Even the Creator stepped back and enjoyed, with praise, the good work he had brought into existence. As sharers of God's image we must copy the patterns God shows us. One model is to take time to enjoy and to dance with full-hearted thanksgiving in celebration of the events, people, and productions God has brought into our lives.

"**A**nother birthday party," I sighed. I was reading an inter-office memo inviting me to eat, drink, and be merry on behalf of one of my colleagues. My mind quickly scanned possible excuses or conflicts that would enable me to legitimately be absent so I could go on with my work.

Celebration is not a comfortable or familiar activity for me. It represents a gap in my response system—a gap I want to bridge as I realize God calls us to be celebrative people.

Times have changed. In the fifties, when I played high school and college basketball, I occasionally pulled off a sensational pass or shot. Crowds cheer cool moves, but I, the momentary hero, constrained by overdeveloped mores of modesty, exhibited no joy. No smile, no exchange of high fives or low fives, no somersaults of happiness, no fist in the air. Just a straight face, a business-as-usual, back-to-work, this-is-serious demeanor. Exulting approached pride, a deadly fault in my catalog.

Today expressions of joy and satisfaction abound in the arena of sports. Handstands, back flips, ball spiking, prancing, and dancing provide a hilarious creative ritual following touchdowns and goals in football and soccer. In fact, many teams are now banning such demonstrations, claiming that they take too much time and easily spill over into taunting the opposition. Maybe the real reason has more to do with the work ethic of NFL officials who, like me, can't stand much frivolity.

Early in life, an inhibiting message infiltrated my brain. It said, "Do not make a big deal of your accomplishments." The ramifications of this creed were that one did not talk about successes, or only with dispassionate brevity. Overstepping these folkways meant receiving a light, verbal-slap warning, "Now don't get a big head." Celebrating victory was a dangerous activity in which one flirted with despicable arrogance. Humility, the godly virtue, required subduing nearly all happy dances connected with achievements.

One perennial festival that most people enjoy is academic graduation. However, my own graduation ceremonies from high school and college were less than joyous events. There were unforgettable events on those days of celebration, but not the kind one usually wants to remember. Only the passing decades have moved these memories from disappointments to comedies.

I was motherless at the end of my high school career. Lacking a mother's guidance, I showed up at the church for the commencement ceremony with my robe still tightly, but handily, packed inside the paper wrapper it had arrived in. To my horror, and the shocked gasps of my classmates, when I opened the package, the robe emerged as a long wrinkled crunch of synthetic cloth that I had no choice but to wear. That's the kind of thing nightmares are made of.

College graduation was another landmark embarrassment. This grand occasion was held in the expansive Civic Auditorium in Grand Rapids, Michigan, with a massive crowd of families and friends in attendance.

The mistress of ceremonies explained we would walk in, two by two. The pairing occurred randomly as two single lines coming from opposite directions merged at the rear of the hall. Fate was unkind. I found myself—a skinny, 6'6", 179-pound geek—side by side with the most petite—4'11"— woman in the class. As we slowly strolled, it dawned on me that the ripple of giggles and laughter running through the crowd was about us. A tide of warm, red self-consciousness surged through my entire upper body as I slunk to my seat. Subsequent graduations—my own and others—nearly always churned up some uneasy feelings dating, no doubt, from these events of old. Contaminated with old sourness, these celebrations remained a chore for a long time. Now, finally, they trigger great chuckles.

Graduations were not my only problem. Birthdays, anniversaries, Father's Day, Valentine's Day, and most of the other special days, with the exception of Christmas, have for unknown reasons loomed as burdensome necessities rather than exciting events.

But now I've changed my mind. I've finally realized that life needs more celebration, that celebrating is fully as important as hard work. I'm certain the Lord gets bored with all our somber industriousness and dances joyfully with us when we do.

Let us not infer too much from Jesus having gone to a wedding in Cana. But he was there. He joined in with obvious energetic concern for the success of the party rather than spending the day teaching or healing. Clearly, the celebration of special events is consistent with the life and spirit of Jesus. Remember how he endorsed the palm-waving, praise-shouting crowds on that day we call Palm Sunday? Long-faced seriousness is certainly not our full-time duty. Joy must break through conspicuously and frequently. God's people have reason for joy.

Birthdays, anniversaries, graduations, and the like are measurable evidence of God's blessings. Another year of life is a gift worth pausing over and a time for firing up some candles of thanksgiving. Marriage too—fraught with pitfalls and challenges, as well as satisfactions and rewards—deserves fireworks of congratulations for each anniversary year of growth and deepening.

Properly most of these celebrations focus on "the birthday boy," a married couple, Mother, the graduate, or an individual marking a special achievement. That's how it should be. Mostly. But if focus on the star is all there is to it, motivation for perpetuating the traditions may run out of gas or founder in the shallows. The electricity for joyous partying should come from being walloped, tickled, or nudged by the profound daily surprise of God's gifts streaming steadily into our reservoirs.

Spending a tad out of the ordinary—even with occasional exorbitance—to make something special of an annual or a once-in-a-lifetime happening is a fitting act of thanksgiving to the Giver of it all. Dancing, singing, shouting for joy over anything great or small is blessed exuberance.

I skipped a couple of my own later graduations, writing them off as unimportant. I was wrong! I have missed birthdays of dear ones, obviously because I didn't regard the event as important enough. I have begrudgingly gotten around to doing something at the last minute for other special days. I am sorry. I'm trying to do better. All of this connects to an erroneous value system—one too lean with reason and practicality, too weak on heart and feelings, too thick with work, too thin on play.

Celebration is so clearly God's idea: "Blow the trumpet . . . strike the timbrel . . . raise a song . . . shout joyfully." God's people of old "twisted," "skipped," and "leaped" in their enthusiastic dancing and merrymaking. I'm not up to that yet, but I'm working on it. Seriously.

SCRIPTURE REFLECTIONS

ROMANS 13:7

Pay to all what is due them—taxes to whom taxes are due, revenue to whom revenue is due, respect to whom respect is due, honor to whom honor is due.

1. Do you pay your taxes and revenues? Have healthy respect for others? Give honor to whom honor is due?

2. Why are we more sure to pay our taxes than remember to give a gift? Remember a court date and not a birthday?

PROVERBS 3:27

Do not withhold good from those to whom it is due, when it is in your power to do it.

1. Give examples of times you have withheld good. What are your justifications?

2. In light of Proverbs, are your justifications valid? Where might you need to make changes?

PERSONAL REFLECTIONS

1. What reasons for joy do you have in your life?

    How are you celebrating them?

2. What are your reasons for being a celebrating person?

    What are your reasons for not being a celebrating person?

    In light of the lesson, where do you need to make a change?

3. Call someone and wish him or her a happy birthday.

    How did the person react?

    What were your feelings?

4. Find an occasion to buy a gift and deliver it in person.

    What was the receiver's reaction?

    What were your feelings?

5. Celebrate something you like about yourself or a personal occasion. Buy yourself a soda or an ice cream, or even take yourself to dinner. Invite a friend—that's a party! Tell him or her what you are doing.

    What was your friend's reaction?

    How are you feeling?